SICK AT SEA

by Mary Winn Heider
illustrated by John Joven

The oddest thing ever to happen to me was in 1747. It was the year I turned 13.

All my life, I had lived on the coast of Scotland. I saw the waves crash on the shore. But I longed for more.

I joined the crew of a big ship. We left dry land and sailed the soupy blue sea.

I took a mop to the decks. I mended the sails. I went to the top of the tallest mast. From there, I felt as if I could see the entire world.

We had been at sea for a few months when I started feeling sick. The crew spoke of men who went mad from sickness, so I pretended to be fine.

But soon I could not ignore it. My gums started bleeding. My tongue hurt. A tooth fell out. I had no energy.

I had dreams about eating fresh foods, such as lemons. Sometimes, I even had dreams while I was not sleeping. I felt as if I could taste the foods, but my stomach stayed empty. The sickness was fooling my mind.

I was spooked.

The first mate said he had a cure. He said that my body missed dry land. So he made me take a dirt bath.

I did not feel better.

The second mate said he could fix me. He said the air down below was bad. So he made me sleep up on deck.

I did not feel better.

Slowly, the sickness struck other healthy men.

A doctor on board had an idea. His name was James Lind, and he was from Scotland, too.

He told us, "I think your food is not digesting properly. This may be why you are getting sick. I think I can help. Who will take part in a test to find a cure?"

I was weak, but I lifted my hand.

The doctor gave us different treatments to try. He had a hunch that some foods and liquids with a strong taste may have something in them that could help.

Two men drank seawater each day. Two others had vinegar. Each morning, he gave *me* one lemon. A lemon, just like in my dream.

The others stayed sick. But I got better.

The doctor gave me an exam. Then he gave me a smile. "The lemon must have something the body needs," he said. "I think we have something to celebrate!"

After that, the others got lemons, too. Soon, we were all strong and healthy again.

We went back to mops and sails and masts.

We went back to life on the sea.

The world was so big. And out of everything in the big, wide world, I had been saved . . .

. . . by a lemon.